Outdoor
PHOTOGRAPHY

PORTFOLIO

GUILD OF MASTER CRAFTSMAN PUBLICATIONS LTD

First published 2001 by
Guild of Master Craftsman Publications Ltd
166 High Street, Lewes, East Sussex, BN7 1XU

ISBN 1 86108 233 9

British Cataloguing in Publication Data.
A catalogue record for this book is available from the British Library.

Front cover photograph: After the Storm, by Mark Layton
Back cover photographs, from left: Last Light at Corpach, by Duncan McEwan;
Wolvadan Dune, by Frank Hollinshead; Swallow in Flight, by David Chapman;
Sand Dune in the Evening Sun, by John Dominick

Cover design by Ian Smith, GMC Studio
Original design, Ed Le Froy

Colour separation by Viscan Graphics Pte Ltd (Singapore)
Printed by and bound by Kyodo (Singapore) under the supervision of
MRM Graphics, Winslow, Buckinghamshire, UK

CONTENTS

INTRODUCTION

A seal pup lies quietly on a lonely stretch of beach in Lincolnshire; the soft light of late autumn caresses a line of boats moored on Derwent Water; a snow-capped Ben Nevis looms above a mist-covered sea loch; the rapid flight of a swallow is caught by a split second of flash.

The above scenes are descriptions of photographs you will find in this book. They are a random selection, taken by dozens of different photographers at different times and places, for a variety of reasons. The one thing these pictures have in common is that they have all appeared in the Portfolio pages of *Outdoor Photography*, taken by the readers of this distinguished magazine.

Seen together in this unique book, the pictures assume a more eminent scale and purpose: they become a tableaux of nature's domain at moments of no apparent consequence, but by their taking and printing these images provide the viewer with insight and experience that would otherwise have been missed.

These days, we take photography for granted because it seems to have been around forever. And yet, the photograph has become the most powerful means of communication of the past 100 years. It is the nearest we have to a universal language. The growth of photography's usage and influence is staggering when you consider that at the beginning of the twentieth century, newspapers didn't carry photographs on a daily basis, magazines were rare, and the whole concept of the printed picture on a page was limited to a few plates in books. Books like this were a distant dream.

The very best photography is always something to treasure. That is the ethos behind Portfolio – it is an anthology of landscape, natural history and travel pictures that gives pleasure to the viewer. The images succeed because each photographer takes an obvious delight in their pastime and reveals a genuine affection for their subject. This success and enjoyment multiplies when the pictures can be appreciated by many more. And when you consider that most photographers were first inspired to pick up a camera after seeing a particular picture or photographer's work, who is to say that leafing through the pages of this book will not move another reader to take those first steps towards a similar goal? If you do feel so moved, at least you will know where to send your pictures first!

I do hope you enjoy this book, and my thanks to all the photographers and readers who co-operated in such a commendable spirit to make it possible.

Keith Wilson
Editor, *Outdoor Photography*

CLIFF SEABROOK

The difficulties of balancing a photographic interest with fulltime work is something most readers of *Outdoor Photography* can relate to. However, this beautiful kingfisher portrait, by Cliff Seabrook of Sevenoaks, proves that the two can work side by side. 'I'm a member of my local wildfowl reserve, and they know me quite well, so when I saw kingfisher activity and asked to set up a hide in an area normally out of bounds, they gave me permission,' he says. Because of his job, he could only spend time in the hide during the early mornings at weekends. As there were no suitable perches in the designated spot, Cliff had to set up one of his own, and keep his fingers crossed that the kingfisher would co-operate. 'Luckily he played the game! I spent four or five hours in the hide the morning I took this shot, and because of the light I was able to use Velvia – its saturated colours meant this was one of the best shots from the session.'
Canon EOS 100 with 300mm lens, Velvia, f/8 at 1/60sec, Benbo tripod

OP verdict **A classic portrait of this dazzling bird, captured in perfect light, and with no distractions in the background**

Some people go on holiday – others take pictures. While the rest of the tourists on the Greek island of Zakynthos were sleeping, Tony Pioli was getting up at sunrise every morning to photograph a small colony of nemopterids which he had discovered in the sand dunes. 'They are quite jumpy creatures, but less so around sunrise and sunset,' he says, explaining his reasons for setting the alarm clock so early. 'It was worth it, because this shot has turned out to be one of my most successful wildlife images and has won quite a few awards.' Spending most of the time lying flat on his stomach, he strove for an uncluttered background which would not distract from the delicate features of the insect.

Olympus OM4 with 135mm lens and extension tube, Sensia 100, 1/125sec at f/5.6

OP verdict Perfectly composed and focused image, showing that perseverance always pays in the end!

RAYMOND FRANKLIN

This magnificent elephant hawk moth is just one of many that Raymond Franklin has photographed over the years. You could call him a bit of an obsessive on the subject. As well as having bred the creatures himself, he has also photographed them in the wild, as was the case with this specimen. 'It was in a field near to my home in Buckinghamshire, and allowed me to catch it and just hook it onto the flower – it sounds sneaky, but we're all guilty of it!' Raymond used a piece of dark fabric rigged up as the backdrop, 'because the elephant hawk is a night moth, so the purists like to see it in dark surroundings.' The rest is just down to natural light – he didn't even have to use the shaving mirror he carries around to double as a reflector. Raymond, who is a member of Amersham Camera Club, is known on the competition circuit for his photographs of moths and dragonflies, and gained his ARPS with a panel on the subject.
Nikon camera with 105mm macro lens, Kodachrome 64

OP verdict An arresting photograph, with beautiful combination of natural colours and textures

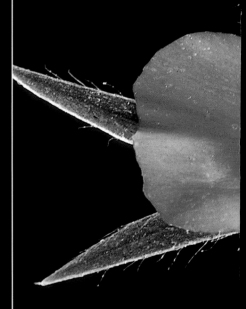

This stunning shot of the Salar de Uyuni salt lake in Bolivia, was taken at sunset by Richard Packwood. The trip to this sea-levelly-challenged country was something of an impromptu decision by Richard and his nephew, who had intended to spend four months in Brazil. Arriving there, however, they found the currency had changed, and it was extremely expensive. 'So we decided to spend a month or so in Brazil, then make our way to neighbouring Bolivia, which was a fraction of the price.' It was while staying in the town of Uyuni that the two of them got together with four others to take a four-day Landrover trip to the salt lake, which is on the border of Chile, at 18,000 feet. This is where Richard can give you an idea of the size of the lake: 'We drove across it for a whole day, and you couldn't see anything but the salt flats in all directions.' And there is a simple, yet entertaining, reason for the success of this picture. It's all thanks to two of the other travellers on the trip. 'Because of the altitude, and on the recommendation of the locals, we were all chewing liberal quantities of coca leaves,' Richard explains. 'There were two mad American doctors on the trip with us who, at the moment I was taking this picture, were doing a crazy, coca-induced war dance, declaring the photograph would definitely be a winner!' And it is.

Nikon F4 with 20mm lens, Velvia, exposure not recorded due to coca-induced distractions...

DTP verdict A beautiful study in light, colour and texture, with a surreal, almost lunar landscape feel to it

There are occasions when all you need for a great landscape photograph are mountains, lakes and incredibly clear air. And New Zealand has all three in abundance. 'My wife Joy and I spent 12 days on South Island last year, which is a stunning part of the country,' says Julian Parton. 'It's a haven for the landscape photographer.' Apparently the climate can change very quickly and the morning temperature can be as low as minus two or three degrees. 'I took this picture around 6.30pm, when the light was beautiful. It's this light and the clarity of the air which make for wonderful scenes that just stretch out before you.' This range of mountains is, quite appropriately, named the Remarkables.
Bronica ETRS with 40mm lens, Velvia, 1/2sec at f/11, polariser and grey grad

AP verdict The crispness of the atmosphere is conveyed beautifully in this image, which makes the most of the lovely light

It was while Malcolm MacGregor was in Sutherland in Scotland copying out locations for an exhibition he was planning that he took this shot. 'The light in Scotland has an indefinable quality – you have to see it, feel it and let it move you,' he said. After he had been there for about three days he spotted a 'rock wall' on the south side of the mountain Quinag. 'That afternoon I could feel something was going to happen; clouds were moving across the sky with shafts of light.' He took some shots of the 'rock wall' and then something made him turn around and he saw a magnificent sight. 'I was so mesmerised by the sudden light that I could hardly think, and only had time for two different photographs before it was gone. When the film came back from the lab I was amazed. I could not remember the dramatic cloud formation that gives the picture depth and balances with the fiery hillside.' The whole event was over in two minutes – never to be repeated.
Mamiya 7II with 50mm lens, Fuji Velvia, 1/8sec at f/22, Gitzo 1228 tripod

OP verdict Rustic colours and a sense of an oncoming storm have combined to create a dramatic composition in one of Scotland's remotest regions

CHRIS LANE

Chris Lane was in the Dominican Republic for his brother's wedding when he found time to spend a day in Manatee Park taking shots of wildlife – all of which turned out to be disappointing. But right at the end of the day, just as he was leaving, Chris put his hand on a wooden handrail and saw right beside him this small lizard which was little more than 15cm long. He knew right away that it was the shot he wanted and had to move fast to take it before it scurried away within minutes. It turned out to be one of his very favourite shots.
Canon EOS 50 with Sigma 105mm macro lens, Fuji Sensia 100, 1/60sec at f/4

OP verdict **Critical focusing, an iridescent colour and a sharp angle give this picture great impact**

Kevin Woods knows how to go about making the most of a nature subject – he buys it as a pet! This tree frog was part of his family for a couple of years, living in a large, heated tank and being fed various live delicacies. The reason for the unusual purchase was because Kevin used to give a lot of slide shows for local nature groups. 'This particular picture was taken to show off its toe pads, and was quite easy to take – I just built the set and introduced the frog onto the tree trunk.' The only slight problem that Kevin occasionally faced was in finding the creature – at only two inches long, it was very good at hiding itself! Nowadays, however, his photography is rather different. Living in Lancashire, he is close to some of the UK's best landscape, so spends a lot of his time shooting mountaineering images instead.

Bronica ETRSi with 100mm macro lens, Velvia, 1/250sec at f/11, two flash heads

OP verdict A slick, stylish image which draws attention to the frog's smooth texture and characterful features

DAVID CHAPMAN

David Chapman has a photographic environment to make any wildlife photographer jealous, as he explains: 'My wife and I have a five-acre smallholding where we keep a few animals. There's a wild area where I have a semi-permanent hide set up, so I can just sit there and wait to see what comes along.' For this photograph of the cheeky-looking long-tailed tit, he put out some bait, and tied the goat willow twig to a post in the ground. 'I was trying to get some backlit shots to emphasise the yellow goat willow, but for this frame the sun was behind a cloud. It turned out to be the best picture, because the others were too contrasty.' David, who is head of the maths department at a secondary school, plans to give up the teaching profession in the near future to turn his hand to full time wildlife photography – he's well on the way! *Pentax MZ-M with Tamron 300mm f/2.8 lens on Kodak Ektachrome E100VS; 1/125sec at f/4*

OP verdict
Beautifully framed and captured, this composition is made all the more successful by the use of the willow branch

Believe it or not, this pin sharp photograph was taken without a tripod! Glynn Maynard, of Haywards Heath, has built a hide in his back garden, and it was from here that he took this photograph of the hungry blackbird. 'You name the bird and it comes to my garden. I just put out the bait and wait to see what happens,' he says. 'I can be very patient if I have to be!' The hide is in a fixed position, but gives him enough room for manoeuvre to cover a wide area. 'Although this picture was taken in the late afternoon, I tend to find early morning is best for bird photography, but I just go into the hide whenever I have a bit of spare time.'
Nikon F90X with Sigma 400mm f/5.6 lens on Sensia 100;
1/125sec at f/5.6; beanbag

OP verdict The late afternoon light shows up the glossiness of the blackbird's feathers perfectly

MICK RYAN

Sometimes the chore of carting your camera with you all day is made worthwhile, as Mick Ryan of Scunthorpe discovered on a walking weekend in the northern part of the Lake District. 'The light was continually changing, but as the clouds moved the shafts of light kept hitting the wrong part of the valley.' However, keeping his camera to hand, Mick waited, and his patience was soon repaid. 'Suddenly it all came right, and it was panic stations to get a picture! I only had time to make three exposures before the light changed again, but I had a gut feeling it would be a good photograph.'
Pentax ME Super with 40mm lens, Agfachrome 100, 1/125sec at f/16

OP verdict: **This is the reason why everyone should carry a camera with them at all times! Perfect timing and patience have paid off, with dramatic results**

STEPHEN HALL

Stephen Hall is lucky enough to live just an hour's drive from this spot on the Lincolnshire coast, where seals come onto the beach to breed each year. This particular pup would have been very young when this picture was taken, as its mother was close by and they only hang around until the pups are three weeks old. 'They are quite curious when they're young,' says Stephen, 'and this one came pretty close to the fence which divides the onlookers from the seals.' An English Nature warden is on site at all times, because the location can get very crowded, and not all visitors are as thoughtful as they might be, letting dogs off their leads and allowing them to run free. 'I visited the beach four times, and on each occasion just followed the seals with my lens, absolutely captivated by them – they really are beautiful creatures.' Stephen, who works in the Jessops store in Lincoln, has decided to make the jump to full-time photographer in the not too distant future, concentrating on British landscapes and wildlife for the time being. 'I'll work on this country until I can afford to go to hotter places!'
Canon EOS 1N with Sigma 170-500mm lens at 300mm, Fujichrome Astia, 1/125sec at f/5.6, monopod

OP verdict **A classic animal portrait, well-exposed and a successful result of perseverance**

RAY VINE

Ray Vine could probably be described as a fanatic when it comes to the late Derek Jarman's house and garden at Dungeness in Kent. 'It's unique, and provides an ever-changing picture in terms of its flora and fauna,' he explains. 'Plenty of others have copied his style subsequently, but he was probably the first person to make use in an artistic manner of the debris left on the shingle.' Ray visits regularly throughout the year to record the changes in the garden, and this picture was taken during early winter, when it looks particularly sparse. He was drawn to the circular formation of stones, with the purple and green plant growing in the centre, so used a wideangle lens to emphasise it, while creating a sense of balance with the distant house. 'It's both artistic and fascinating in the way it is presented,' he concludes.
Nikon F5 with 24mm Nikkor lens, Kodak Gold 200, 1/125sec at f/16

OP verdict A great combination of forms, which has been photographed in the ideal light to bring out the subject

Curtis Welsh describes himself as a very keen amateur who always has a camera by his side as a constant companion. He has travelled widely to places like India, China and Vietnam to pursue his photography. This beautiful shot of Derwent Water was taken a little closer to home, but is, none the less, still impressive. Using the golden light of late autumn, Curtis has produced an image that perfectly captures the mood of the location.

Bronica ETRSi with 40-90mm lens, Fuji Provia, grey grad

Winchelsea Beach, near Rye in East Sussex, is a favourite photographic hunting ground for Sittingbourne-based Ron Edwards. 'I always find something down there,' he says. 'It's a great place for photography.' Something of a specialist in close-ups of detail and texture, he is always on the lookout for images such as this one. 'Believe it or not, I didn't set up this picture at all,' he continues. 'The tide had just gone out, leaving this shell high and dry on the groyne, and the late evening sun picked out all the textures and ridges perfectly.'
Canon EOS 100 with 100mm macro lens, Velvia, 1/8sec at f/22; Benbo tripod

OP verdict: **A well-observed image which combines texture, tone and light to very subtle effect**

RICHARD PACKWOOD

'A stunning failure,' is how Richard Packwood describes his attempts to photograph the 'big things' in Canada's Jasper National Park. But while the elk, moose and bear – among other creatures – were less than co-operative, he did learn a lesson from these ravens. 'It taught me that you mustn't ignore the smaller animals.' The ravens were sitting on a crash barrier in a lay-by, so Richard stopped the car to take a closer look. 'It's very difficult to get close to ravens in the UK, but these two were just hanging around, and let me get out of the car and set up my tripod before taking the picture. They probably sat there for about 15 minutes in all!' A semi-professional photographer, and pharmacist by trade, Richard spends as much time as possible photographing wildlife and natural history subjects, travelling on a freelance basis as often as he can. *Nikon F5 with 300mm lens, Provia 100, 1/30sec at f/5.6*

OP verdict A lovely character portrait of these two impudent looking birds, enhanced by the soft light and muted colours

JOHN POTTER

The intriguingly named Smaws Ings is a small group of trees in Tadcaster, North Yorkshire, close to where John Potter lives. It's an area he knows well, having grown up there. 'I always make a point of getting in the car and driving there if it looks like there's the possibility of a good sunset,' he says. The beautiful colours you see here are the result of the afterglow which follows a sunset, and to balance the light with the foreground, John used two grey grads, while retaining the lone oak tree's silhouette. Although it was shot on a 6x6cm format transparency, John decided afterwards to crop some of the sky from the top of the image in order to anchor the tree more strongly in the frame. *Bronica SQA with 50mm lens, Velvia, eight seconds at f/11*

OP verdict **The purple tones of the sunset's afterglow provide a perfect backdrop to this simple silhouette**

JOHN POTTER PHOTOGRAPHER e-mail: j.s.potter@btinternet.com   website: www.jpotter-landscape-photographer.com

LEONARD LAPKA

After Leonard Lapka's first holiday to Namibia, under the tutelage of Charlie Waite, he decided that he'd had such a good time and learnt so much that he wanted to repeat the experience. Back in that magnificent country he found himself no less in awe of its stunning scenery. 'It is incredibly impressive and is not like any landscape I'd ever seen before,' he said. 'The best thing for me was this red sand – it had little touches of iridescent green in places, from small amounts of vegetation. It was almost indescribable, the colour and the sheer vastness of it.'

The team had set out before sunrise and stood a long time in the cold waiting for the sun to edge its way up inch by inch. 'Coming from Florida I really felt the cold, but it was worth the wait,' said Leonard. 'I learnt a lot from that holiday – not least of which was a taste for gin and tonic!'
Minolta 600SI with 28-105 lens, Velvia, 1/30sec at f/8

OP verdict **If you go with Charlie Waite, get up at dawn and it's Namibia, you really can't go wrong!**

PAUL WHITING

If it's Tuscany, it must be one of Charlie Waite's Light and Land holidays! That's certainly the case with this classic view of the incredibly photogenic region, which Paul Whiting, a software project manager for Nokia, took during the first day of his holiday in May 2001. 'You can shoot it from the road, but really it's far too dangerous,' explains Paul. 'So instead, Charlie was good enough to drive us across the fields in order to take the shot – although it was a hire car he was wrecking!' Only having a short time, Paul was immediately attracted to creating a long view with a wideangle lens, with the green fields providing the foreground interest. 'The light was very subtle at that moment, and the trees have an abstract quality when set against the sky and expanse of wheat,' he continues. Paul, who is thinking of going to Andalucia next year, enjoys the courses for the talking as much as the picture-taking. 'I've been on Light and Land breaks to the Lake District and the Peaks, and have found the conversation and exchange of ideas to be as beneficial as the actual photography.'
Hasselblad 501CM with 50mm lens, Velvia, 1/4sec at f/32, 0.45 ND grad and polarising filters

The coast of southern California is one of the most beautiful stretches of shoreline in North America. Facing west, it means that whatever the time of year, a sunset over the expanse of the Pacific Ocean is guaranteed. Just north of San Diego is the trendy village of La Jolla. It has a sandy beach, surfers and some wondrously slender palm trees that line the headland above the shore. Keith Wilson stayed here a few days and photographed the sun's descent into the ocean at the end of each day. This was one of Keith's favourites because the line of palm trees creates a gentle curving lead-in line to the centre of the picture. *Contax 159MM with 25mm wideangle lens, Fujichrome 100, 1/125sec at f/11*

OP verdict: **The contrast of orange and blue sky, and the silhouetted figures, convey the balmy warmth of the sunset**

MIKE KEEGAN

Abbotsbury Swannery in Dorset is one of those places that has, over the years, become something of a Mecca for wildlife photographers. Mike Keegan is one such fanatic, and as such tries to make a trip from his Bedfordshire home at least once a year. This dramatic shot was taken around July time, when the swans lose their flight feathers. 'Because they get frustrated at not being able to fly, they flap in this dramatic manner, and I'd spotted this pair on a number of occasions.' Mike deliberately set a slow shutter speed to blur their movement and create a sense of action, a technique he uses a great deal in his photography. 'It's fantastic when it works,' he says. 'But it's very much hit and miss, and is an expensive way of taking pictures. You can use up half a dozen rolls of film, but only get one or two successful pictures from them.' And as he has recently retired, he is coming under a bit of pressure to save money. 'I'm getting my wrists slapped – I'd better start using flash!' *Canon EOS 5 with 75-300mm IS lens, Provia 100, exposure not recorded*

OP verdict Vibrant and immediate, this shot manages to be both graphic and abstract at the same time

JOHN DOMINICK

In this beautiful shot of a sand dune near Chichester Harbour, John Dominick has taken maximum advantage of the low evening sun to bring out the texture of the sand and grass.

'Although I travel a lot within the British Isles, this shot was taken in my home county and is an area I know well,' explains John. 'For this particular image I used an 81B warming filter to enhance the mood and also a 0.6 graduated neutral density filter to hold detail in the sky.' A photographic shop manager by profession, John is naturally drawn to the land both through his work and his photography. He prefers working on the west side of the country, where he feels the landscape and quality of light offer the best photographic oppotunities.

Bronica ETRSi with 50mm lens, Fuji Velvia with 81B and 0.6 neutral density filters

OP says The quality of light has turned a fairly mundane subject into a striking image

With the usual tremendous effort required, Dave Robertson heaved himself out of bed very early one cold winter's morning, as the weather forecast the night before had boded well. 'It turned out exactly as I had hoped,' Dave says. The picture shows a memorial stone, which stands at a visitors' centre near Thornhill in Stirling. 'I had seen it in the past and knew it would make a good dawn subject,' he continues. 'And this was my first attempt at photographing it! It's pretty unusual to succeed first time around.' Knowing he wanted to frame the stone as a silhouette, Dave took a meter reading from a mid-tone area of the sky. This helped to retain detail in the distant mist. 'The whole shoot took about half an hour from arriving to unpacking – I was running a little late as usual, so it was all a bit of a rush!' *Mamiya RB67 with 360mm lens, Velvia, one second at f/16*

OP verdict
Perseverance and an early start have paid off, as this mystical stone would appear rather ordinary in bland lighting conditions

Sunrise at the spectacular Zion National Park is definitely the best time for photography, as Nick Higham discovered on a trip there in May 2001. 'Not only is the harsh, late morning light too contrasty for the red rocks, but by mid-morning it is too busy with people for photography.' After seeing a picture of a ponderosa pine perched on a rock in a travel guide to the area, Nick was on the lookout for something similar with which to make his own interpretation. 'My wife spotted this one, which was very close to the road, so easily accessible.' Readers may recall that May 2001 was the time of the great fires across the USA, so conditions were far from ideal for photography. As Nick puts it: 'This part of the world is so wonderful, though, it's hard to go wrong – you can almost guarantee good pictures, whatever the weather.'
Minolta 800si with 24-85mm lens set at 35mm, Fuji Superia 100, 1/90sec at f/11

OP verdict A very successful graphic image, with lovely contrast in colour and texture

SIMON BOOTH

There's nothing like having a co-operative subject to help your wildlife photography, as Simon Booth of Chorley discovered on holiday in Florida this year. 'I went specifically for the bird photography, and found this brown pelican resting on the beach at Sanibel Island,' he says. 'It was very approachable, so gave me the opportunity to try out various angles. The downward sweep of the bird's feathers made me decide to crop in tightly.' Simon, a machine operator by trade, who takes pictures every spare moment he has, always tries to bring an element of artistry into his wildlife photography. However, he has had mixed responses to this picture. 'Some people love it, while others – the purists – have criticised it for chopping the frame in half. It's one of my favourites, though!' You can expect to see Simon's name more regularly in future, as he hopes to turn to photography full-time within the next couple of years.

Canon EOS 100 with 300mm f/4 lens, Provia 100F, 1/180sec at f/8, fill flash set at -2 stops

OP verdict **A bold interpretation and crop, which concentrates attention on the texture of the bird's feathers, and is completed by the sparkling eye**

JOANNA MUFFET

Joanna Muffet's father inspired her at a young age with a love of gardening. 'I was brought up with muddy fingers, sowing seeds and taking cuttings,' she says. It was a combination of this lifelong interest and a newly acquired interest in photography that led her to take this picture. 'I started taking photographs in October 99 when my partner bought me a camera for my birthday. I only take shots of plants and flowers and occasionally gardens and landscapes. I thought it was important to concentrate on one thing only and try and get it right,' she said.

The photograph of this crown imperial (Fritillaria imperialis) was taken when the conditions were just right – good light and no wind. Joanna said: 'I particularly liked it because of the contrast of colours and thought the orange would work well on the Fuji Velvia. I also liked the pollen which was oozing off the stamens. I was lucky with this particular flower as I was able to isolate the umbel.'
Canon EOS 300 with Sigma 105mm macro lens, Fuji Velvia, f/32, tripod

OP verdict A good and accurately exposed shot with well balanced usage of flash

This stunning flower is one of many to be found in Sheffield Botanical Gardens, a location David Severn visits frequently. 'It's a fantastic location for photography – particularly if you're interested in flowers and close-ups.' When he took this photograph, he had just bought a new camera and lens. 'I decided to head for the gardens to spend a bit of time getting to grips with the new kit,' he says. 'The brightness of this particular flower was a real pull, so I just took as many pictures as I could, and hoped!' *Nikon F90X with Tamron 90mm macro lens on Sensia 200; 1/30sec at f/16*

OP verdict David did the right thing by isolating this handsome flower against a dark background, to make it really stand out

A successful photograph often relies on a combination of being in the right place at the right time, a touch of local knowledge, and a splash of stunning light. Duncan McEwan, of Bridge of Weir, found all three as he was driving up to Fort William for a short break last winter. 'It was late afternoon and the sun was going down. I was lucky to capture the last hint of light, which gave the scenery a very calm, misty feel.' Avoiding the classic view of Ben Nevis from the Caledonian Canal, Duncan instead drove about a mile further on – there was just enough time – to Corpach, where he knew he would be able to capture the scene he was after. 'The tide was out, so I tramped over the muddy shore, where there was a choice of boats to give a middle-distance focal point. I chose this one because of its orange buoy, which gave a hint of colour to the scene, as well as mirroring the colours of the sunset.'

Mamiya RZ67 with 110mm lens, Velvia, 1/4sec at f/16, no filters

OP verdict A stunning yet subtle monochromatic scene, with depth and a composition which brings together its elements perfectly

Unlike many underwater photographers, Morris Gregory started off with a passion for picture-taking – the diving came later. However, about 10 years ago, when his wife persuaded him to accompany her on a diving trip, he was hooked immediately. 'I'd been a keen photographer for many years,' he explains. 'So naturally I wanted to begin taking pictures of the underwater world as soon as possible after I became qualified.' Nowadays he manages to get away once or twice a year, often abroad – although he doesn't shun the colder waters of the UK. 'I enjoy the challenge of taking photos in British waters, even if it is cold and sometimes it's difficult to see more than a metre or so in front of you!' This particular picture was taken in somewhat warmer climes – Borneo, to be precise. The creature is a ghost shrimp, and it was on some bubble anemone. Originally our dive guide had spotted an orangutan crab, and had beckoned me over to take some photos. I fired off a couple of shots, but it was half-buried in the anemone and just looked like a hairy, orange blob, so I concentrated on this nearby ghost shrimp which, to me, was much more photogenic.'

Nikon 801S with 50mm lens in Subal housing, Sensia 100, two Ikelite strobe flash units

DP verdict An intriguing study in underwater life, where the background is as fascinating as the shrimp itself.

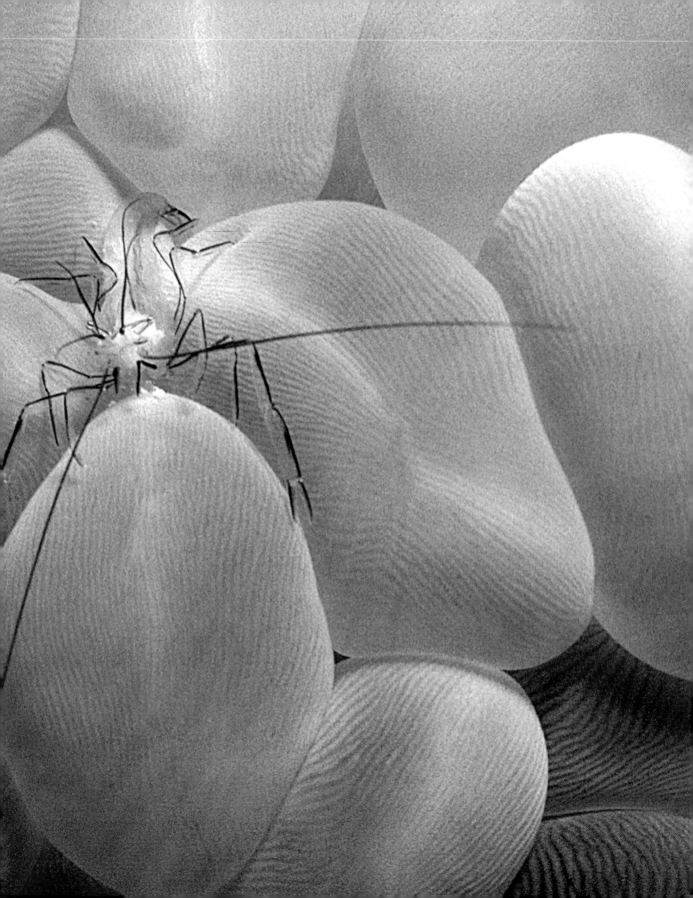

David Chapman is lucky enough to have a smallholding, which he has spent time developing into a wildlife haven. Many of the birds and animals which are attracted to it become subjects for his camera. Such was the case with this swallow. 'They were nesting in the barn, so I set up a flight tunnel, with the aim of photographing them using flash. After a few rolls of film, though, I decided I wanted to try photographing them using natural light.' To achieve this, David set up a hide at the end of the tunnel, because he had seen that the swallows would hover there before they flew in. 'I was only able to shoot eight or nine pictures, and didn't even have time to focus. It was a combination of luck and judgement.' This was the only chance he had to photograph the swallows, as it was late in the season and the birds soon left. As they have visited the barn for the past few years, hopefully they will be back again next year, bringing with them more opportunities for photography. *Pentax MZ5N with 300mm f/2.8 Tamron lens, Sensia 100, 1/250sec at f/4*

OP verdict A picture which perfectly reflects the speed of the swallow. Well previsualised and composed – luck or no luck!

TOM RICHARDSON

Many readers of OP combine their passion for photography with a love of walking, and Tom Richardson is a case in point. He is often to be found making his way across the fells and dales of northern England, and his photograph shown here was shot on an old peat road in Eskdale, to the west of Scafell in the Lake District. 'It was the middle of winter, and was blowing quite a strong wind, but I didn't have a tripod with me so I braced myself against a fence post to get the picture sharp.' The light was very fleeting, constantly changing between dark stormclouds, and fingers of sunlight stabbing through. The clouds were moving so fast, he only had to wait a few minutes before the elements came together for this shot. 'I love this area of the lakes, it's very wild, and completely different from the "pretty pretty" shots you often see of the region.' *Bronica ETRS with 50mm lens, Velvia, 1/60sec at f/8, grey grad and 81B warm-up filters, Manfrotto tripod*

OP verdict A wild, moody image, reflecting the tension which exists in the Lake District's climate

Believe it or not, this stunning photograph isn't the only successful shot in a strip of 20, taken after a day spent stalking a herd of wild Dartmoor ponies. The truth – that would make most of us green with envy – is that Robert Maier, of Ravensburg in Germany, was driving close to Haytor on Dartmoor, when this stallion appeared racing through the bracken. 'I had my camera in my hand and had to move very quickly – I could only take one shot before he was gone.' And if you've ever handled a Pentax 67 camera, you'll know that moving quickly doesn't come too easily. Robert comes to Britain every year for three or four weeks, and admits to envying British photographers for the wealth of wildlife that's found here.

Pentax 67 with 400mm lens, Provia 100, 1/500sec at f/4, monopod

AP verdict **Not bad for a grab shot! Captures the grace and character of the pony perfectly**

Mike Rhodes, of Wetherby, is a braver person than many of us. The reason? This picture was taken during a camping trip to the Lake District in January 2001. 'It was so cold, the water was freezing inside the tent!' Mike says. 'But at least it meant we were able to get up for the best light, rather than being restricted to the breakfast hours in a guest house.' On the day he took this image, there was perfectly crisp, clear light, and this turned out to be just one of several successful pictures shot that morning. 'I was just in the right place at the right time for the light,' he says, 'as it's the reflection of the reeds that makes the shot.' And the reason the Canada goose was in this particular spot was simple – it was the only part of the lake that wasn't frozen over!

Canon EOS 5 with 170-500mm lens at 170mm end, Kodak Extra Colour 100, 1/60sec at f/8, Benbo tripod

OP verdict **A simple yet effective composition, which comes together thanks to the lovely early morning light**

'I was just walking past this owl at Marwell Zoological Park,' says Phillip Gould, 'when she turned and looked into the bright sunlight. It was one of those completely spontaneous and lucky shots photographers like so much, but which only happen rarely!' Phillip, who lives in Southampton, makes a point of always taking the photograph, even if they don't all turn out exactly as he'd hoped. 'The most important thing is at least to try, and if it doesn't work out, you only end up wasting a frame or two.'

Canon EOS 50E with Sigma 400mm lens, Sensia 100, aperture priority at f/5.6

OP verdict: An unusual treatment of a popular subject, the shafts of natural sunlight and a shallow depth of field complete this shot of the captive owl

IAN CAMERON

If you fancy seeing a sunset like this, first you need to be made redundant from your job – and so receive a financial windfall – then just head for Pra Ngan beach in Thailand. That's what Ian Cameron did. 'It was part of a two-year trip round the world, which took me through South Africa, Zimbabwe, Nepal and Australia, as well as Thailand.' he says. 'I stayed there for about three or four weeks, and the skies just glowed this incredible colour at twilight. On this particular night, there was a perfect crescent moon high in the sky, so I needed a wideangle lens to give it the appropriate sense of space. The boat sat perfectly the bottom third of the frame.' Ian is now back in the UK and working as a police constable in Scotland, but still travels when he can. 'You have to keep your feet on the ground but your head in the clouds!' *Contax RX with 28-85mm lens, Provia 100, 1/4sec at f/5.6, 81B warm-up filter*

OP verdict **Beautiful muted tones, with the crescent moon completing the tranquil atmosphere**

This photograph is a fine example of why it is worth revisiting an area time and time again. Rarely is it the same twice. On the day Mark Layton took this picture at Burton Bradstock in Dorset – a regular haunt of his – there had been a strong storm. 'I had never seen the beach like this before,' he says. 'The storm had swept away all the shingle and stones which normally cover the area, leaving the whole ledge exposed.' He explored the beach for a suitable rock pool to use in the foreground, and fitted a wideangle lens to emphasise it. 'You can only photograph this area successfully in January, as this is when the sun sets over the sea. The rest of the year it sets behind the cliffs.' And of course, the sunset has to coincide with low tide, but don't get too carried away with your photography... 'After I took this picture, I turned round and saw that the tide was coming back in again quite rapidly,' says Mark. 'I had to pack up my camera and hurry the half-mile walk along the beach to make it back to high ground before I was cut off!'

Mamiya RB67 with 50mm lens, Velvia, one second at f/22, sunset and polarising filters, Benbo Trekker tripod

AP verdict A stunning scene, capturing the raking light perfectly, and anchored by the foreground rockpool

IAN CAMERON (top)   ADRIAN EVANS (bottom)

These two palominos, who live in a field off the road between Inverness and Loch Ness, were only too happy to be photographed. In fact, their curiosity actually hindered the picture-taking process, as Ian Cameron explains: 'I didn't have to follow them around for a long time in order to get them in the right place. They took one look at my camera and headed straight for me. In fact, the problem was keeping them far enough away to take the picture!' Ian moved to Scotland a few years ago, and is a police constable in his home town of Forres. 'I'm lucky because my beat coincides with the best scenery in the area, and because I work shifts, I can often get out to take pictures during the good weather. Not many jobs give you that chance.' Best of all, he can see the improvement in his photography since he's been making the most of living in the heart of some of the best scenery in Britain! *Bronica ETRSi with 75mm lens, Velvia, 1/60sec at f/11, 81B warm-up filter, tripod*

OP verdict **A well observed, wintry scene, with the ponies providing a splash of colour against the monochrome backdrop**

DAVID SOUTHERN

When we first saw this shot of the erupting 'Pacaya' volcano in Guatemala by David Southern, we were amazed by the drama of the photograph and also more than a little envious of David's luck in being there at the time. However, as the saying goes, you make your own luck and this can certainly be applied to David and the determination he showed in capturing this striking image.

'This volcano is in a mountain range about 40 miles from Guatemala City. I had read in the local paper that this particular peak was expected to erupt and was very keen to photograph it. There were no official excursions to the volcano, but some local people were offering to lead parties up a neighbouring peak that afforded the best view of the eruption. To reach the summit we had to trek for two hours through rainforest and hills that are notorious bandit country. Our vantage point was itself a volcano and the hot ash that we were standing on made my tripod legs too hot to touch. It was then just a case of waiting for the decisive moment.' After this remarkable photographic excursion the party had to find their way back through the rainforest by torchlight.

As head of IT at the World Wide Fund for Nature, David feels a strong affiliation with the natural world and describes his photography as 'a real passion'. He and his wife travel regularly to Central America and are currently planning a trip to Cuba.
Canon EOS 10 with 28-135mm lens, Fuji Velvia, 'a slow shutter speed' at f/8

OP says A never to be repeated picture, the result of determination and plenty of initiative

Tresco is one of the five inhabited islands of Scilly, situated off the tip of Cornwall. It is a beautiful island surrounded by clear blue seas more reminiscent of the Aegean than the Atlantic. There are no cars on Tresco and the 150 inhabitants get around by bicycle, so you can imagine what a gentle and relaxing pace of life it is here. The coastal scenery is spectacular and with the island being small enough to walk around you can easily follow the light from one side to the other. Cromwell's Tower is on the northwest of the island and, in this photograph by Keith Wilson, it is bathed in the warm evening light of April, just half an hour before sunset. 'The wind was gusting in from the Atlantic,' says Keith, 'so I had to add ballast to my tripod by tying on my camera bag!'

Pentax 67 with 45mm f/4 wideangle lens, Velvia, 1/8sec at f/22, tripod

OP verdict: The rocky foreground leads the eye perfectly down to the tower, their texture enhanced by the sidelighting of the late afternoon

The stretch of North Antrim coastline where this photograph was taken is one of Jonathan James's favourite photographic spots. 'There's an incredible range of scenery – from volcanic rock to limestone,' he explains. There's some gorgeous light, too. 'On this evening, the whole of Northern Ireland was cloudy, but it stopped dead at the cliffs and was completely clear out to sea.' He continues: 'You take pot luck with Irish weather. Sometimes it's so good you can get a dozen good pictures in a day. Other times you won't get a thing for a fortnight – very frustrating!'
Kowa Super 66 with 55mm lens, Velvia, 1/8sec at f/22, no filters

OP verdict A tightly composed scene which makes the most of the gorgeous light, and is anchored by the pink flowers in the foreground

RICHARD PACKWOOD

Taken on Great Saltee Island, a privately-owned bird sanctuary off southeast Ireland, this picture is a double exposure combining the moon and the birds.

Richard Packwood explains: 'We had obtained special permission to camp on the island and this photograph was actually taken around 11pm. Although the moon was casting this beautiful light on the sea, it was too high in the sky to be included in the same frame as the birds,' explains Richard. 'I first made a two-minute exposure of the birds with a 50mm lens. I then used a 300mm lens and changed my viewpoint slightly to photograph the moon at 1/30sec. There is probably a bit of reciprocity failure involved, but I think that adds to the atmosphere.'

Richard, a pharmacist by trade, regularly contributes to the Oxford Scientific Films Picture Library. *Nikon FM2 with 50mm and 300mm lenses, Kodachrome 64, double exposure at two minutes and 1/30sec*

OP says A stunning picture borne by the photographer's ability to previsualise the result and bring together the elements of the scene for a successful result

s a chartered surveyor for Northwest Water, and based in
endal, Matt Baker gets out and about in some of the UK's
veliest landscape for his work. But he doesn't stop there.
keen fisherman, he regularly goes sea trout fishing with his
ther to the North Harris estate. 'When fishing, there's very
ttle chance for photography, so I decided to return in August
f this year, specifically to take pictures and to try to do
stice to the outstanding photogenic scenery of the Western
les,' he explains. On the day he took this picture, Matt
rrived at Seilebost beach, on South Harris, around mid
orning. Impressed by the views out towards North Harris,
e set up his camera to include the foreground flowers –
nown in the isles as Machair – as well as the stunning
each and distant islands. To the left of the image is the
noreline of Taransay, recently made infamous by the BBC's
astaway programme. 'I stopped right down, to make sure
verything from the flowers to the hills was in focus, and I
ook advantage of a lull in the wind – a constant factor in
his part of the world!'

entax 67 with 75mm lens, Velvia, 1/4sec at f/22,
olariser, tripod

P verdict **A picture so vivid you can almost smell the sea air!**

RACHEL SIMPSON

This lighthouse can be found at Byron Bay – the easternmost point in Australia. Rachel Simpson stopped here during the couple of months she spent driving from Sydney to Cairns. 'It's a huge tourist attraction because the coastline is so amazing,' she says. With the aim of creating a feeling of being led up to the lighthouse, she composed with the sweep of the fence in the frame. 'Because it's so popular, especially at dusk, I had to wait for ages until there were only a few people in the shot.'
Centon 300 with 28-70mm lens, Velvia f/11 and 1/60sec

OP verdict: A strong composition which leads the eye into the frame in exactly the way intended, and she has made the most of the wonderful lighting

Frank Fell is a much travelled photographer specialising in architecture and landscape. He sells his work through photo libraries in both London and Sydney. This beautiful shot of the Singapore skyline was taken last year on a trip which Frank describes as part holiday and part work. 'The weather was very cloudy during my stay and there was a lot of building work going on at the time, so I felt night-shots would offer the best photographic opportunities. I decided to use a tungsten balanced film to enhance the blue of the sky and a long shutter speed to capture the light trails of the boats crossing the harbour,' explains Frank.

Canon EOS 1N with 24-85mm lens, Fujichrome 64T, 30sec at f/22

OP says A fine example of astute film use and exposure control for a crisp, colourful result

JONATHAN PHILLIPS

'It's often reported that Antarctica is going to be closed off to tourists, so I thought I'd better go there while I still had the chance,' says Jonathan Phillips. 'I knew nothing about photography, but thought I should take a decent camera with me, and I came back with about 700 pictures!' This image was taken in Chilean-claimed territory – the Madonna is their religious icon. 'I was drawn to the way one penguin seemed to be quite curious about the Madonna, while the other wasn't taking any notice.'
Nikon F50 with 28-200mm lens, Provia 100, programmed exposure

OP verdict: A cleverly captured comical moment, taken from an angle which suits a subject as small as a penguin

While on holiday on Scotland's Ayrshire coast, James Craig sat on the beach at the town of Girvan, taking photographs of the island of Ailsa Craig as the sun set behind it. 'I knew they weren't really working out' he says. 'So I waited until well after sunset and took my shot then – keeping the sunset filter in place. Actually, it was a complete accident, as I didn't realise the colour would turn out like this!' James does not own a car, so has to rely on public transport or a bicycle for his picture taking. 'As a result, I'm always in places at the wrong time of day for photography, so it's always a bit of a happy accident when something does work out!'
Canon EOS 5000 with 38-76mm zoom at 38mm end, Velvia, exposure not recorded, sunset filter and tripod

OP verdict Clever observation of a subtle scene, with great use of a tricky filter

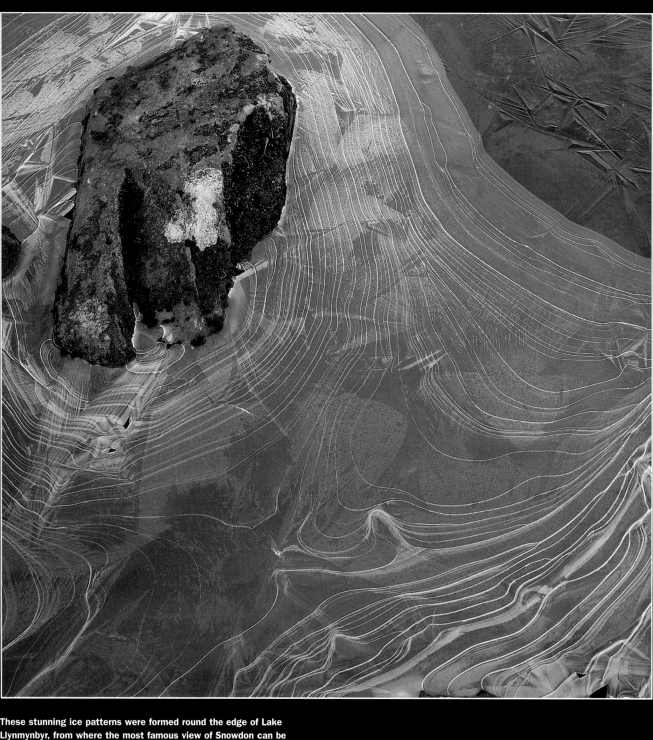

These stunning ice patterns were formed round the edge of Lake
Llynmynbyr, from where the most famous view of Snowdon can be
photographed. Pierino Algieri lives a mere 15 minutes from the spot,
so is a frequent visitor, especially during the autumn and winter. 'After
a hard frost, the edges of the lake freeze in these swirling patterns,'
he says. 'But it happens rarely and only lasts a short time before
melting.' Pierino always keeps an eye out for the formations, and
treads very carefully in his search for them. 'The ice is very thin,
and there's water underneath which forms the patterns, so it's easy
to tread on and break up the ice before you realise what you're doing.'
He can see the Snowdon mountain range from his window, so has the
luxury of rarely wasting a trip with his camera. 'I never get bored with

To Paul Richardson, this picture represents a triumph of optimism over laziness. 'I'm just not capable of getting up at the crack of dawn, even with the promise of excellent light for landscapes in the early morning. Consequently, like most of my photography this was taken at the worst possible time – early afternoon in July.'

These cliffs are to be found a short distance from Dieppe on the Normandy coast at Veules-les-Roses. Living near Newhaven in Sussex, France is only a couple of hours away for Paul, who exploits day-return ferry tickets for trips with his camera.

'I was initially attracted to this scene by the way the overhead sun emphasised the cliff's colour and texture, particularly against the rich blue of the sky. Having composed the shot, my only regret was its rather static nature – then a gull came to my rescue, forming the classic outstretched shape at the top of the cliff at the moment of exposure.'

Olympus OM1N with 28mm lens, CrystalArchive print from a Velvia transparency, f22, polariser

OP verdict: **Very effective use of a wideangle lens to create a balanced image out of very simple elements. The solitary gull adds a focal point to the scene.**

Just because a particular photographic subject is popular, it shouldn't prevent you from trying to photograph it yourself. This was Craig Roberts' plan when he visited some relatives in Harrogate last winter. 'I spent a day photographing the northeast coast from Scarborough to Whitby, and started off here at Saltburn Pier. I had seen a lot of pictures of it before, but had never visited it myself.' Arriving at sunrise, he chose his viewpoint quickly – mainly because it was extremely cold – and waited for the sun to appear. 'At first I didn't think I was going to get the picture, because it was so cloudy, but suddenly the sun broke through for a very brief time. Then it went again, but the cloud stayed!' It was a financially successful day, too, as later on Craig was photographing a beach scene at Scarborough, when a passer-by asked him for a copy of the picture he was taking! Mamiya RZ67 with 50mm lens, Velvia, 1/8sec at f/16, 81C warm-up filter and 0.6 ND grad

OP verdict Proof that light is what lifts a photograph above the ordinary, this picture has a wonderful sense of space

If you can rely on one thing when photographing in Scotland, it's that the weather is never the same from one moment to the next. Edinburgh-based Ian Browning was on a camping trip in the Highlands last April – 'it was freezing!' – which he used as an opportunity to try out his latest photographic purchase, a 6x6cm Mamiya C330 twin lens reflex. 'The weather had been miserable all day, and I'd been trying to take pictures around Glen Etive, with no luck. Just before we headed off, we thought we might as well take a look at Black Rock cottage and, as we pulled up in the car, there was a sudden break in the clouds.' Alan rushed to set up his camera, using the rocks in the foreground to balance with the distant mountains, and pull the eye into the frame. 'I had time for just three frames before the light went again. And then the film sat in the camera for two months before I had the chance to develop it!' Pleased with the results, he has gone on to use the camera more and more regularly. 'I love the square format. It can be tricky to find subjects which fit it, but when a composition works, it's great.'
Mamiya C330 with 65mm lens, Fuji Neopan 400, two seconds at f/22, lightly sepia toned

OP verdict This very well-known cottage lends itself effectively to the square format composition, and is made doubly moody by use of black and white

This particular badger sett is one of several which Colin Sargent of Tavistock photographs each year. And it's a particular favourite as it's in a very isolated position, so his hard work and patience isn't thwarted by people walking their dogs through the area! 'Badgers are very very shy animals, so I set up my gear while it's still light and pre-focus on one of the entrances to the sett,' says Colin. 'Unfortunately, they are also unpredictable, so if they come out of a different entrance it's too late to do anything about it!' Despite this, he still describes the sight of a badger's nose appearing to sniff the night air as 'magic.' Although he works fulltime at the Ambrosia dairy, Colin still finds time not only for his photography, but also to judge competitions, give talks at camera clubs and even, last year, to appear on television! 'Because of my job, I find the typical British weather extremely frustrating. If it's bad I have to wait until my next day off before I can take any pictures.' And that's something we can all sympathise with!

Minolta 7000i with 70-210mm lens, Sensia 200, 1/125sec at f/11, two off-camera flash guns, hide

OP verdict Patience and perseverance has paid dividends, for a picture which has more than just the 'aah' factor

PETER CLARK

'I took this photograph at Friog beach in North Wales,' says Peter Clark of Cannock. 'Having seen plenty of pictures of streams and waterfalls taken using long shutter speeds, I wondered how it would affect the sea, as the water moves differently.' He fitted a polariser and red filter and, after compensating for reciprocity failure, arrived at a shutter speed of 30 seconds. Having already shot a lot of film at this location, he only saw this shot out of the corner of his eye as he was leaving the beach. 'I had to work fast as the tide was going out, and only had time for four or five shots before it had gone too far.' But it was worth it, because the print then went on to be his most successful picture, and is exhibited regularly at national and international salons.

Canon EOS 1 with 28-70mm zoom at 28mm; Ilford Pan F rated at ISO 25; 30 seconds at f/32 with red filter and polariser

OP verdict
A cleverly pre-visualised image, with a subtle, ethereal feel

FRANK HOLLINSHEAD

This sensational photograph of Wolvadan Dune was taken while Frank Hollinshead, of St Ives, was on a Light and Land photographic holiday in Namibia. 'We were heading back towards the camp – which was in the middle of the wilderness – when we drove over the top of a dune and saw this scene before us,' he explains. The trip had been organised to coincide with the end of the rainy season, as the skies are much more dramatic at this time. However, the storm brewing on the horizon of this picture meant they had only a short time to photograph before the guides were ushering them back into the Landrover. 'Then the most almighty storm blew up!' Frank continues. 'Thunder, lightning, torrential rain – you name it. But at least I got the picture!'
Nikon F5 with 20-35mm lens on Velvia; programmed exposure and polariser

'Like being on the surface of Mars,' is how Geraint Tellem
describes the experience of standing at the summit of
Haleakala, the volcanic crater which makes up most of the
Hawaiian island of Maui. During this enviable holiday, he rose at
3am, to ascend the volcano and be at the summit in time for
sunrise. However, this picture was taken a few hours later. 'At
the actual sunrise there was not so much to take, but three or
four hours later, the interior of the crater was bathed in light, and
the weather conditions were changing every few minutes – the
place has its own micro climate.' Because of the relative lack of
people, the crater also had a silence unlike anything Geraint had
ever experienced. 'I've never known anything like it. I'd
recommend anyone to go to Maui – there's so much to see, it's
impossible to keep your camera in your bag.'
*Mamiya RZ Pro II with 90mm lens, Velvia, 1/125sec at f/8,
polariser*

OP verdict **An almost surreal vision, which brings out the sheer
scale of the crater**

When we first saw this picture on the lightbox in the OP office, we were convinced it was a close-up of lichens on a rock, designed to have the appearance of snow-covered trees. However, on phoning Alan Clark to find out a bit more about the picture, we learned otherwise. 'It was taken last year during a trip to America with Nigel Turner Photo Holidays,' he explains. 'There had been a snowfall, and we went to photograph the sunrise. Then these trees in the distance caught my eye.' Yes, these trees were several miles away and, when the view was compressed through the 300mm end of a telephoto zoom, the 3,000ft cliff face behind them created a highly dramatic backdrop. The tour took Alan round several of the canyons in the area, introducing him to areas he had not visited before. When at home in the UK, he tends to shoot landscape, nature and sport subjects, 'you just have to travel a bit for it!'
Canon EOS 5 with 75-300mm lens, Agfachrome 100, 1/60sec at f/11

OP verdict A real optical illusion on a staggering scale, perfectly executed to create the trompe l'oeil

Barry Amos, of Canterbury in Kent, was in the middle of hanging wallpaper when we called him! But he took the time to tell us a bit about this bold composition of the famous limestone pavement in Malham, North Yorkshire. 'I had seen this place in photographs many times,' he says. 'And it's definitely somewhere I would go back to. I always look for a strong foreground interest, but on this occasion I deliberately selected a shallow depth of field to draw attention to the rock formations.' Unusually for a landscape, Barry took this picture in the middle of the day, when the sun was directly overhead. 'I thought in this case it helped, because it brought out the detail in the foreground.' *Mamiya RB67 with 50mm lens, Velvia, 1/250sec at f/8; polariser and tripod*

OP verdict: **A confident picture that breaks the rules that say landscapes should be taken with maximum depth of field, and at the beginning or end of the day**

'I was waiting for someone to turn up with the keys to let me into our camera club meeting, so I took a few pictures to pass the time,' explains Nick Jarvis of this unusual image of a teasel. This angle is characteristic of his work. A member of the Disabled Photographers' Society, he can only walk short distances. 'As a result, a lot of my photography is taken either kneeling or sitting down, therefore I take lots of pictures at a low level looking upwards!' The teasel was lit with a small Lastolite foil reflector, hence the very crisp lighting on the plant. 'I felt the bright sky would look good, and was just lucky that the clouds came together as a backdrop,' he says. *Canon EOS 3 with Tamron 90mm macro lens, Kodak EBX, f/16, Lastolite reflector*

OP verdict An unusual perspective which brings out the spiky texture of the teasel, framed perfectly by the sky

'This is one of my favourite spots for photography – and it's about as close as you can get to the Millennium Dome,' says Geraint Tellem, who lives in south London and can reach the much-maligned structure with relative ease. 'It was only possible to get the shot on a Sunday morning, as that's the only time the roads are clear enough to get there quickly,' he continues. Luckily this particular Sunday morning had all the right conditions, including a clear sky and no breeze – essential for a perfect reflections – and he reached his spot on the

project? 'I was there on the opening night, which was very impressive despite what people said. And I did get in for free, so I can't really complain!'
Mamiya RZ Pro II with 90mm lens, Velvia, 1/8sec at f/16, magenta filter

OP verdict A modern structure such as this one cries out to be photographed in perfect symmetry, and the filter completes the futuristic feel

TOM RICHARDSON

Tom Richardson is, like many a photographer, a huge fan of the Lake District. However, he prefers to stay slightly off the beaten track, in particular by exploring one of the many Mosedales, just south of Loweswater. 'This was taken on one of those days where there was a lot of cloud, with occasional bursts of sunlight,' he says. 'It was ideal for the isolated, open sort of shot I like to take.' Tom, who was Ilford Printer of the Year a few years ago, spends as much time in the darkroom as he does out in the landscape. 'With monochrome you obviously don't look for the subtleties of colour, but you look for texture and the play of light – in this case in particular on the reeds to the right.' *Nikon F90 with 28-80mm lens and orange filter, Agfapan APX100, developed in Agfa Rodinal and printed on Kentmere VC paper*

OP verdict **Black and white was the ideal choice for this scene, as it reveals the shapes and textures in the landscape**

This double exposure was shot on tungsten balanced film, which is what gives the sky its rich blue colour. Philip Hawkins lives in Edinburgh, so knows the city extremely well. He headed up to this vantage point on Carlton Hill, looking west along Princes Street, with the specific intention of making a double exposure. 'I just waited for a full moon on a clear night and went there, which is one of the four good hilltop locations for photography in Edinburgh.' First he made the street exposure, framing it with enough space in the sky. Following this, he made the moon exposure. 'I placed it in the top right of the frame as I thought it would balance well with the face of the Balmoral Clock,' he explains. And, as Princes Street is always busy, he didn't even have to wait long for cars to provide the traffic trails.

Canon EOS 50E with 75-300mm lens for moon exposure, 28-70mm lens for street scene; Fujichrome 64T tungsten balanced film; 1/60sec at f/11 for the moon, 45 seconds at f/16 for the street scene

OP verdict **Patience and forward planning are key to a successful double exposure of this kind**

As with most keen hillwalkers, Stephen Street and his wife venture out in all sorts of weathers and, living only two hours from the Lake District, Cumbria is a much-visited region. Never leaving the house without his camera, this photograph shows Great Gable, a couple of miles northeast of Wastwater, on a particularly nippy winter morning. 'I don't know what the air temperature was,' says Stephen, 'but the wind chill was severe – around minus 10-15 degrees! When I stopped to take the picture, my wife had to carry on walking just to keep warm.' Sheltering in the lee of a crag, Stephen set up his Mamiya C330f, taking a spotmeter reading from the brightly lit snow and setting this to expose as the highlight area of the image. Although the Mamiya is bulky, he finds it is no weightier than his Canon EOS 3 kit. 'I hang it around my neck, then clip it to my rucksack, and don't even notice it's there.'

Mamiya C330f with 80mm lens, Provia 100, 1/8sec at f/16

OP verdict **Captures the atmosphere and sheer cold of the day in a successful square-format composition**

It took Billy Stock a number of visits to the New Severn Bridge before he finally took this shot. 'The bridge doesn't look good in the daytime,' he said 'so I had to keep going back to find the right light. It was of course complicated by the tide times because I wanted the reflection of the bridge in the water. There are a couple of mud flats in the picture but they don't seem to detract from the reflection.'
Billy used a graduated filter because the water was much darker than the sky. He is a great believer in bracketing widely. 'It would be terrible to have the light and the tide and everything just right and then walk away having not got the right exposure!'

He is also a great believer in really knowing his subject and being patient enough to wait for the moment when all the elements come together. 'I always go back again and again to get the right shot,' he says.
Mamiya 645 with 150mm lens, Fuji Velvia, 20sec at f/22, 0.9 graduated filter

OP verdict Judicious cropping of the 645 format has emphasised the symmetry and angle of this perfectly exposed twilight scene

Below **Steve Clarke took this photograph while visiting his son on the Isle of Man. 'We walked down a small country lane to a cove and then thi cottage suddenly came into view – it stood out so magnificently that I just couldn't resist taking the shot,' he said.**

Steve has been an enthusiastic photographer since 1988 when he got his first SLR. He enjoys taking landscape shots as well as black and white portraits of jazz musicians. 'They are two very different types of photography but I enjoy that contrast – I think it keeps me fresh,' he said *Olympus OM4 Ti with Zuiko 35-70mm lens, Fuji Provia 100, 1/25sec at f/8*

OP verdict **A well considered composition enhanced by moody lighting that gives an almost three dimensional effect**

Although John McCann lives in lovely Perthshire, he has relatives in the north of England, who he visits regularly. On the way back from one such visit, the weather was looking promising. 'It was one of those afternoons, around 2.30pm, so I diverted from the normal road and took the Clyde Valley Tourist Route instead. I came upon this scene and just knew I had to have the shot.' As John knows the area well, he was able to predict that the light would be good on this day. And he has a certain fondness for this part of Scotland. 'This is a particularly attractive valley, and is beautiful in summer or winter. It's not your typical Scottish landscape, either. It's much more rolling, and has a totally different feel altogether from other parts of the country.'

Nikon F801s with 28-200mm Tamron lens set at 180mm, Velvia, 1/8sec at f/16, warm-up filter

OP verdict A scene which makes the viewer want to don scarf, gloves and walking boots, and climb the mountain!

This lovely waterfall is the Crackpot Falls – we kid you not. Harry Wentworth was out driving one day, and stopped in the hamlet of, appropriately enough, Crackpot, to see if there were any photographs to be had. 'I heard the sound of water, so I scrambled down a bank and found this waterfall,' he says. 'It was a dull day, and I didn't want to go home without a photograph, but weather like this is ideal for shooting running water.' Harry, who lives near Leeds, has recently started exploring the North Yorkshire moors – which is where the charmingly-named village and its waterfall can be found. *Canon A1 with 19mm lens, Velvia, 1/15sec at f/8; tripod*

OP verdict: **An atmospheric monochromatic scene, which has translated onto film very well. The choice of shutter speed isn't so long as to lose the drama of the running water**

Andy Darrington always makes a point of visiting Richmond Park during the deer rutting season, which is when this picture was taken. Arriving fairly early, he was lucky enough not to have to work too hard for this image – he simply stepped out of his car and there, over the road, was this obliging stag. 'His attention was obviously elsewhere at the time, but you still have to keep an eye on them because they can come after you if you're not careful!' As a result, he fitted a 400mm lens and 1.4x converter to his Nikon D1 digital camera, allowing him to keep his distance. Andy has owned the D1 for a year now, and is very pleased with the results he is getting from it. 'It's great for wildlife, and because it takes Nikon lenses, it fits in with my existing kit. Best of all, I can go home after shooting and download my pictures straight away.'
Nikon D1 with 400mm f/2.8 lens and 1.4x converter

OP verdict A well-timed image, where the photographer has waited for just the right angle to show off the perfect antlers on this magnificent stag

Being a somewhat shy, retiring creature, a harvest mouse picture such as this one, by Andy Darrington of Potton, would have been somewhat tricky to set up in the wild. So when he found his cat had cornered one in a five-gallon drum, he rescued it and, in return, the mouse modelled for him. 'I set up a glass tank on the kitchen table,' he explains, 'then made a background and placed some corn in the centre of the tank, before introducing the mouse.' Using two flash units – one either side of the tank – to light the creature evenly, and a third to light the background, all Andy then had to do was wait for it to strike a pose. After the photo session was over, the mouse was released into Andy's five acre smallholding – a haven for wildlife and, inevitably, wildlife photography. His next photographic project is with the badgers that moved into a hole he had dug only a week earlier. 'We're hoping they might breed there this year,' he says. *Nikon D1 with Tamron 90mm f/2.8 lens, two Nikon SB28 flashguns and one SB27 for background*

OP verdict **Despite being photographed in captivity, the mouse and its surroundings make an extremely convincing image**

When the sky is grey and there's no chance of the sun making an appearance, it's still no excuse to sit inside thinking about what sort of pictures you could take if the weather was better. Just do what Simon Stafford did for this picture – fit a macro lens and pop into the back garden to see what reveals itself. 'Rather than shooting a bog-standard flower portrait, I decided to close in on this tulip's pattern and detail, just scanning the lens around the flower to see what happened,' he says. 'This diagonal pattern of the reds and yellows just fell into place.' The exciting aspect about macro photography is that the world it reveals is very easily accessible. As Simon puts it: 'It's just a question of getting down low!'

OP verdict A simple macro image which has impact thanks to its two contrasting colours, and because of the diagonal composition

GARY HACON

Gary Hacon drives a lot for his work, and as a result is constantly on the lookout for potential photographs, which is how this picture came about. 'I was driving along and noticed that the farmer had obviously left this verge untouched so that the poppies could grow,' he says. Parking the car and walking back, he knew there was potential for a good picture, so he framed carefully, ensuring the horizon was perfectly straight. 'Rather than actual landscapes, I'm usually more on the lookout for graphic shapes, which is exactly what I saw in the straight lines of this scene.' *Nikon F90X with 24-120mm lens at 28mm on Astia 100; 1/60sec at f/11*

OP verdict This picture goes to prove that the simplest compositions can sometimes be the most effective

GARY HACON

When looking for photographic subjects, Gary Hacon is drawn to images that will have a strong graphic feel. Simple uncluttered photographs are the hallmark of his work.

'I rarely photograph anything in its entirety,' explains Gary. 'I prefer to move in close and pick out detail that one might not see in the wider view. I always use a tripod and will often push the film stock to its limits, using very long exposures, to produce the image I want'. This particular photograph was taken at dusk during what were the last few minutes of available light. Shortly afterwards the sky was black, making photography impossible.

Nikon FE with 50mm lens, Fuji Velvia

OP says A well composed composition that stands out for its simplicity and contrast variance

'The weather was so bad this day, I really didn't think I'd get anything,' so says David Phillips of this stormy image. He had set off from his Carlisle home that morning just with the intention of walking in the Ullswater area, and despite the weather, he still took his medium format kit with him. 'I knew this burst of light, giving a contre jour effect, happened occasionally, but I certainly wasn't expecting it.' However, at around 11am, the sun burst through for a brief spell, giving David just enough time to set up his camera. Despite living in the midst of this spectacular scenery, he finds it increasingly difficult to photograph the area. 'It's so over-photographed – and is photographed so well – that finding somewhere new is actually harder than going somewhere less photogenic to take pictures.' Nowadays, when he does venture into the

Greenland is a vast mass on the map, covered in an ice cap three miles deep and with a rugged coastline that remains frozen nine months of the year. Keith Wilson took this picture on a trip to the east coast in April, staying in the town of Angmassalik. At this time of year, you can only get around by dog sledge or skidoo. With so much snow and ice around, and with a clear, unpolluted sky, the sunlight is quite intense. Sunglasses are essential to avoid snow blindness.

Taking accurate exposures in these conditions is very tricky – it is such a harshly lit environment. To convey that harshness in this picture Keith decided to give prominence to the sun and include the resulting flare as well. 'You can't spotmeter in a situation like this,' says Keith. 'Just take an average reading and then overexpose by a stop. The one thing that you can't sense from this shot is the immense silence of the landscape. The only thing you can hear is your breathing – and that of the dogs!'

Canon T90 with 20mm f/2.8 lens, Kodachrome 64, 1/500sec at f/16, +1stop exposure compensation, polariser

OP verdict: **A tremendous sense of space is reflected in this sparse, cold image**

Cameron Struthers has had a lifelong passion for boats and shipping. 'My father worked in shipping and he used to take me along to see the boats – and that was it, I was hooked,' he

'The end of April is the best time for tulips,' says Mani Puthuran of Holland – where else? A doctor at Hull Royal Infirmary, he keeps busy in his spare time by taking pictures, preferably during trips abroad. 'I'm building up my portfolio of travel work, with the aim of submitting a selection to a photographic library eventually,' he says. This trip to Holland was very successful, and Mani made a point of visiting this particular area. 'Apparently it is one of the last places where there are a large number of working windmills. People still live in the houses underneath them.' He headed there at sunrise in order to capture the windmills at their most photogenic, and used a warm-up filter to enhance to glow of the early morning sun.

Mamiya RB67 with 50mm lens, Velvia, 1/2sec at f/16, 81B warm-up filter

OP verdict Subtle, early morning light brings out the best in this timeless scene

The thing that Keith Wilson likes about London Docklands, is that the skyline is always changing. It is a living, moving urban landscape. Keith captured this view of Canary Wharf and a mass of construction cranes in the low light of a November afternoon in 1999. Of course, in the two years since this picture was taken, two more skyscrapers the size of Canary Wharf have been built next to the landmark, drastically altering this view from South Quay. 'I like the softness of the light – the sun's low slung trajectory in late autumn makes this a good time to photograph this area, and I keep coming back', says Keith.

Voigtlander Bessa L with 43mm wideangle lens, 1/125sec at f/16, Provia 100

OP verdict: **An interesting juxtaposition of tradition and modernity, with some lovely warm light on the side of Canary Wharf**

MARK BAUER

When we telephoned Mark Bauer to find out more about the carnival of colour that makes up this photograph, he did his best to find out exactly which part of the New Forest it was taken in. However, his 15-month-old son, Harry, was having a great time in the background, doing his best to destroy Mark's map of the area! Nonetheless, we can be fairly certain that the picture was shot in a part of this picturesque forest known as Rockford Common, near to Linwood. And despite sharing the care of his son with his partner, Mark still has time for successful photographic trips, as this image demonstrates. 'I took it on an early morning trip in late August,' he explains. 'I know the area fairly well and was pretty certain that the colours of heather and bracken at this time of year would be good.' Arriving just before sunrise, this particular photograph was taken just after the sun came up, when the quality of light was still soft, and there was a hint of mist on the horizon.

Pentax 67 with 55mm lens, Provia 100, one second at f/22, light grey grad

OP verdict An atmospheric photograph, where the colour is not all-dominant, but leads the eye to the distant horizon

A regular visitor to the Lake District, Kevin Howchin of Chelmsford recently came to the conclusion that he prefers the area's trees to the lakes for which it is named! This striking image was taken at a deciduous forest area near the River Duddon. 'Normally I wouldn't have taken a picture like this,' says Kevin. 'But that morning I'd discovered that my macro lens had misted up on the inside, so I left it in the car to dry out.' Therefore he was forced to look at the subject differently and, on encountering the spectacular honey fungus, he instantly thought of his 20mm lens to convey the potential drama of the scene. And luckily, I'd come across the fungus while it was at its best, and not three days later – which is what usually happens! I went back to the tree the following May, and by then it was actually dead – the fungus had killed it.'
Nikon F90x with 20mm lens, Kodak Extra Colour 100, 1/2sec at f/22, tripod, silver reflector

OP verdict A bold interpretation of a familiar subject, proving it always pays to look at things from a variety of perspectives

INDEX OF CONTRIBUTORS